What is the matter

with Mary Jane?

*With love for Princess Sancia
and her very own 'happily ever after'.*

WHAT IS
THE MATTER WITH
MARY JANE?

STORY BY SANCIA ROBINSON
WRITTEN BY WENDY HARMER

DRAMATIC LINES, TWICKENHAM, ENGLAND

This book is intended to provide resource material
for teachers in schools and colleges. All rights are
strictly reserved. Applications for amateur
performance licences must be made in advance
before rehearsals begin to:
Dramatic Lines, PO Box 201,
Twickenham, TW2 5RQ, England

Applications for professional performance
licences must be made in advance before
rehearsals begin to:
Hilary Linstead and Associates
PO Box 1536 Strawberry Hills
NSW 2012, Australia.
E-mail: hla@intercoast.com.au.

A CIP record for this book is available
from the British Library

ISBN 0 9522224 4 2

What is the Matter With Mary Jane?
first published in Australia in 1996 by Currency Press
PO Box 2287 Strawberry Hills NSW 2012 Australia

Published in England in 2000 by Dramatic Lines
PO Box 201 Twickenham TW2 5RQ England

Printed by Southwood Press Marickville NSW
Cover Design by Hana & Jana Hartig

The photographs that appear within the text are of the Sydney Theatre Compa
production of What is the Matter With Mary Jane? at Wharf 2, March 199
Photographer: Tracey Schramm.

Contents

What is the Matter with Mary Jane? was first produced by the Sydney Theatre Company and New Stages at the Wharf 2, March 3 1995:

Written and directed by Wendy Harmer
Story by and starring Sancia Robinson
Designed by Daniel Tobin
Lighting designed by John Comeadow

INTRODUCTION

Sancia is posing in front of the mirror... pouting, pulling her hair back, squeezing her pimples and experimenting with a brand new cleavage.

Hello, my name is Sancia Robinson, I am 16 years old and I am a size 10... but it's OK... I know I should be a size 8.

Pleased to meet you... well, I'm not really because I know you are looking at me thinking: 'Boy, what a fat pig... she could sure lose a few kilos... like 50.

You're absolutely right... I busted the zip on my shorts this morning... and I've had those shorts for six years! They're my favourite shorts. Now they're just a skin on a bratwurst sausage.
My mum's trying to tell me it's OK... like I'm meant to be growing. Growing into what Mum? A mutant baked bean?

My whole body is just exploding... I look like an enormous battered saveloy.

Look at my bum. I have a huge bottom... go on... look at it... bean bag bum... Back of a bus bum. Chubby bum... Excuse me Miss Robinson, is that your bum or a whopping big bag of Cheezels inside your jeans? 'Never Miss the Seat Sance' they call me.

In fact, there's only one thing in the world more humungous than my bum and that's my stomach... have a look at this... paunchy, pudgy, roly poly, tubby gut. Spud gut. Old blubber belly. Bag of jelly bean belly.

Have another chocolate biscuit Sance... why not? You already look like a Wagon Wheel... Miss Biscuit Barrel. Miss Monte Carlo. Princess Chocolate Royal. Scone head... hot buttered scone head... with two raisins for eyes.

Check me out... probably the first time you've ever met anyone with Chiko Roll arms, fish fingers and potato wedge legs. You are what you eat, Sance... and your body is a bag of junk. I've got the brain of a chicken nugget.

Two all beef legs,
no neck
huge boobs
fat cheeks.
All on a sesame seed bum.

I'm sorry... what did you say your name was again?

*　　*　　*

Hello and welcome to the show... my name is Sancia Robinson and I am 30 years old and I'm still a size 10... but it's OK.

Of course when I was a little girl I wanted to be a princess... like most little girls, I guess.
Standing at the parapet in my silver gown, diamond tiara, my golden locks ruffled by the breeze... sort of like Claudia Schiffer in a Chanel ad.

Snow White, Rose Red, Sleeping Beauty, Rapunzel ('It won't happen overnight, but it will happen')... I loved those stories. They were ethereal, tortured beauties... angst ridden, falling about in dead faints, locked in towers.

But at the time, how was I to know they were a bunch of neurotic co-dependents with self esteem problems and eating disorders? You have to remember this was back in the days when you couldn't even imagine a Princess using a toilet, let alone vomiting her dinner down one.

I mean, obviously you cannot have a normal life living in a tower. You try ordering a pizza and telling the delivery guy he has to climb up your hair.

She mimes pulling up her hair and opening a pizza box.

I hate pineapple!

Alas and alack... there were no stories about plump post-adolescent princesses.

And no wonder... in fairy tales, even the apples are poisoned!

It was at the age of 16 I could see I was in danger of turning into a fairly ordinary common fat frog. And if I couldn't control the rest of my life... there was one Magic Kingdom of which I was sole ruler. My body.

Happily it was also at the age of 16 I realised I was brilliant at losing weight. I was already a good student. I got top marks in pure and applied maths; physics; chemistry and English. But if dieting was a subject, I would have topped the State.

I went from eight and a half stone to seven and a half in a matter of weeks (that's from 54 kilos to 47 kilos)... an absolute genius! How did I do it? Everyone at school wanted to know.

If you wanted to know about physics you went to Bag Lady Griffiths; English... Rollerball Wilson... but if you required information about the calorie content of a vegemite sandwich, no butter no crust... you came to Sance.
What are you going to be when you grow up Sance?
Hmmm. I can't decide, either Jenny Craig or Gloria Marshall.

Hi... you know, I used to be the size of a pineapple before I went to Gloria Marshall.
My mother and father were always telling me what to do.
Nobody noticed me at school.
I had no life of my own.
I was just ordinary.
And then I lost weight.
Now I am the size of a pea and life is wonderful!
Thanks Gloria!

I could have worked out a diet for Mother Theresa...
'How heavy are you? Seven stone. And how tall? Four foot... hmm.
And you lead a pretty active lifestyle. But, you really do need to lose at least a stone. I would suggest a 1000 calorie a day regime. Breakfast – 3

ounces muesli, skim milk, whole wheat toast and boiled egg; Lunch –
water packed salmon on Ryvita (now make sure you get SeaKist... don't
get John West because that's got less calories), small apple (no more
than 159 grams, so weigh it if you have to). Dinner – 1 cup pasta;
tomato dressing (no oil and I mean absolutely no oil); small green salad
(as much as you like... and just a sprinkling of tomato). And if you're still
hungry after that... maybe a small diet yoghurt, (but just try and have
half).'

Come and see me next week and I'll check your progress.
Ah, Dr Robinson you have such discipline, strength... you are an
example to us all.

Lunchtime was my favourite part of the day... but probably not for the
reasons you think.

'Oh, phew, half an apple! I think it will be a bit much for me!'

While the other girls around me were stuffing their fat faces with bags of
Twisties, pies, sausage rolls.

'Anyone want this last bit of vegemite sandwich... I just couldn't eat
another bite... sigh.'

And the regal, blue-blooded slender Princess Sancia, who was still a size
10, but would soon be a size 8 with long, blonde hair and very long legs
– swooned... the wind blowing her hair into a thousand brave and
dazzling threads. (I read that in a Judith Krantz novel... good hey?)
Well you might not be impressed... but the girls definitely were.

'Oh my God Sancia... you are so thin. You lucky thing. Look at your
arms... they dip in at the top like Kate Moss' arms... they just go straight
down... and your waist... hey everyone, come and look at Sancia's
waist... it's teeny... it's minute... .you must be smaller than Heather
Locklear... and she is like... nothing. What size are you? You must be like
a zero. God I wish I could be skinny like you Sancia.'
Oh come on... I'm not skinny... I could still do with losing a few
pounds...

'No way mate... no... you look just perfect... anything thinner and you would look like... just weird.'

No really... because, when I am skinny...

IN THE MIRROR

When I am skinny...

I'll laugh all the time
I'll be very cool
I'll be in the magazines
And look good at the pool.

The sun will be shining
I'll drive a fast car
I'll meet Ronan Keating
I'll be a star.

My eyes will be sparkling
My arms will be brown
My legs will be long
I'll wear a silk gown.

I'll have loads of friends
I'll never be wrong
I'll be healthy and wealthy
wise and strong.

I'll always be kind
I'll always be nice
I'll always be good
I'll only eat rice.

I'll jog every morning
And run every night
I'll be light as a feather
As high as a kite.

I'll only drink water

I'll live on fresh air
I'll float through the heavens
With the moon in my hair.

Oh God... I think I'm starting to hallucinate.
I must be hungry.
Oh well... only three hours to tea time.

Dieting is divine...

Not only is it the way to a fabulous body... but it's also a miracle cure for everything else that's wrong in your miserable little life.

If you fight with your Mum... you think about lunch.

Hate your brother... how much do I weigh?

Can't do your maths... why did I eat that?

Disagree with your teacher... what did I have for breakfast?

No tears, no pain... everything under control... and... looking good.

AT THE TABLE

OK... Sance... what did you have to eat today? One piece of toast, skim milk for breakfast... 180... let's make that 200 calories... half an apple at lunch, two Ryvitas after school... about 400 calories.

Right... now I know I said we could have 800 calories today, but if you can get it down to 700 you will be under seven stone by the end of the week.

So... I want you to remember that before you sit down... and be careful. Thanks Mum... what is this?

Is this sole fish? Great... (that's got less calories) and did you weigh it? Is it 100 grams? (I bet it isn't. Because it looks like more than 100 grams to me... I'll just cut the end off... yeah, that looks like 100 grams now.)

And you grilled it? And you just put Pure and Simple underneath it.

(She used oil... looks like oil) Did you really use Pure and Simple? Thank you, thank you.

What's this Mum? (Squash... what's she got squash on here for? How many calories has squash got in it? I think it's got 36.)
Mum how much did this squash weigh? (Why didn't she weigh it? I'm not going to eat that, now I'm in a bad mood... why did she do that to me?)
No, I'll just leave the squash, I don't like it. No, I don't want something else. (That'll teach her.)

(God, now I'll be really hungry. I can't eat the fish, because this plate's got oil on it. Carrots, that's OK... wow that's really sweet, she's put sugar in this.)
Mum, did you put sugar in the carrots? (No sugar... these are really nice.)
Yeah, I will have some more carrots. No, no, that's enough... can you take the squash away?
No, I only want to eat the foods I wrote on the list... what did I write on that list? I wrote... beans, cabbage, carrots, cucumber, tomatoes, lettuce and fish... there is enough variety in there for me to get all the nutrition I need. Why did you buy me squash? No, I don't want lemon juice. (That's seven more calories.)

(Do you believe this? She knows I have a bit of a problem with food at the moment, so why is she deliberately going out to upset me?)

No, I don't want dessert tonight thank you.
No, I told you, I don't want meringue. No, I know I used to like them, but I don't now, and don't put it on the table... I don't want to look at it, I don't want to be around it. Now I can't eat my tea, I feel sick that. Why are you doing this to me... now I can't eat my tea.

Put it in the bin, put it in the bin... no, I don't want it for later, put it in the bin.
(See what she's doing to me? She wants me to be fat and ugly? Why? Well, that's it then. From now on I'll do all my cooking and shopping by myself.)

JOGGING

You are a guts Sancia... you are a glutton... you are a pig... sitting up to the trough with your little trotters on the table... snuffling your food like a hairy piglet.

You actually wanted to eat that meringue didn't you?
Wanted to swallow the whole thing.
You would have eaten the plate if you could.
You cannot be trusted.

I will have to keep my eye on you.
I will have to watch you every second of every minute of every hour of every day.

Because you are weak Sancia.
Weak and lazy.
Gross. You are vile.
You are a sinful, pathetic disgrace.
You have no self control.
A spineless coward who wants to give in.

Well that won't happen while I'm in charge.
From now on you are under arrest.
And you will be punished.
You will eat dirt if I tell you to.

Because we are at war.
We are on a long march.
Through hard times.
Through a vale of sorrows.
With an unfavourable wind blowing at our backs
And an evil star at our shoulders.
No pain, no gain kiddo.
Just do it.

Hang on a minute... who are you?
You, of course.

Where are we going?
Six stone.

EXCUSES

Phone rings.

Oh hi Genevieve.
Dinner?
Who's going?
Is it just you and me? Oh everyone's going.
Will there be boys there?
They're not?
Good.
Where are you going?
Pizza Hut.
Oh gee, Genevieve, you know I'd really love to come but...

I just ate.
I'm allergic to cheese.
I was once sick on pizza and I've never been able to eat it since.
I'm a vegetarian.
I promised to have dinner at home.
I can't eat this late at night.
I'm no allowed to eat anything with oil in it.
I'm diabetic.
I've decided I'm not eating any more junk food.
I have some weird stomach bug.
I've just been jogging.
A whole lot of us have decided to boycott Pizza Hut... it's a political thing.
I'm having bowel tests tomorrow morning so I can't eat.
I have to study.
I'm diabetic... Oh, I said that already?
I have to babysit my brother.

I've ground down my teeth so I can't eat meat.
I'm going to the pictures with mum.
I have to wash my hair.
The cat's sick.
Er... I have to wash the car?
I have to rearrange all my underwear in very big baskets according to their size and colour... lots of baskets...

Look Genevieve... I'm just not hungry... OK?
Have a good time.
Bye.

Sancia hangs up the phone and turns her attention to her studies.

I was wondering when I could go out again?
You already go out.
No, I mean out, out.

Well, where?
To a film.
Someone's made a film on year 12 Physics, have they?

Can I go to a party?
I'm sorry, but not with that acne all over your face.
Where?

I can see a pimple.
What about a book or some TV?
If you think you can take time off study it's up to you. I don't care if you fail.

Maybe I'll phone Genevieve.
Who wants to listen to you?
But she is my best friend.
WAS, you mean. Don't you know everyone thinks you're weird?
Well, I was invited on a bushwalk.
Yeah, everyone will get a good laugh at lunch when you pull half a lettuce and ten raisins out of your backpack.

I could fly a kite for a bit.

What use is that to anyone? There are people starving in Africa, you know.

Hey... I could go for a bike ride. That burns up heaps of calories.

Now you're talking... 50 ks should do it.

Hmmm... well, I guess I'll do more study.

What about your sit ups, lazy bones?

Alright, how about I do 250?

Good girl.

But when will I be allowed to stop all this?

When you're perfect.

IN THE TOILET

Well hey, girls... if you can't leave the house... you may as well chuck down a packet of laxatives and enjoy a good night in.

[*bored, looking at back of toilet door*] You know I am so over babies sleeping on pumpkins... I think I might put my kittens in a basket poster back up. [*Sancia picks up 'Supermodel' magazine.*] Of course, if you're stuck in the toilet for 16 years, you can always cheer yourself up by reading 'Supermodel' magazine.

SUPERMODELS! They came as small children from a galaxy far, far away... only one thing can stop them... the dreaded cellulite.

And I love these health tips... from Elle... drink at least two litres of spring water every day.

Come on! Elle could drink water from the toilet and still look good.
I don't even understand why girls want to be supermodels. I mean do you just wake up one morning and think: 'Hey. I know what I want to do with my life... I want to change my clothes 17 times a day and walk in time with music.'
Talk about underachievers!

Oh, here's a great story:

'LINDA EVANGELISTA'S CAREER IN DANGER AFTER EMERGENCY SURGERY'. Apparently she may never model swimsuits again after an operation left a scar on her stomach.
I wonder why they had to operate on her stomach?
Maybe she had a bit of food lodged in there.

And here's another... 'PAST LIVES OF THE SUPERMODELS'.
(You think I'm making this up, don't you? I'm sorry folks... it's right here.)
Hmm... it says here that in a past life Helena Christensen was named Grunder and lived in Stockholm in the 1800s. She was an overweight madwoman who was covered in tattoos and wandered through the city at night screaming and waking up the townsfolk. She didn't always have it so good girls!
I think they mean that in a past life Helena was Roseanne Barr.

Oh look... this is my favourite...

Diary of a Supermodel...

Monday... off to Paris for a Chanel parade.

5 am: Got up, spent two hours examining face for pimples; plucked eyebrows; shaved armpits; waxed legs; changed hair colour; practiced looking bored.

7 am: Ate cornflake.

One minute past seven: Threw up.

Five minutes past seven: Did one thousand sit-ups; caught cab to airport. Accidentally fell down grate in car park.

10 am: Rescued by SWAT team who pulled me out with magnet on my belly button ring. Lucky I didn't get my nipples pierced!

11 am: Wow! Sat next to Mick Jagger in first class... I mean, so what, sat next to Mick in first class...

Five minutes past eleven: Mick fell asleep and dribbled on my Armani jacket.

Spent next 12 hours flying to Paris trying to do crossword.

Hmm... what's a four letter word meaning: 'Any substance containing nutrients such as carbohydrates, proteins and fats which can be eaten by a living organism and metabolised into energy and body tissue?'

Too hard... filed nails instead.

7 pm: Backstage at Chanel... make-up team arrive with sticky tape, Spakfilla, scaffolding, and orbital sander.

9 pm: I've made it! Here I am on the Paris catwalk, under the glare of a million flashbulbs.

10 pm: Taken to Paris hospital with temporary blindness and two detached retinas.

Midnight: A great day. I lost two kilos!

BITCH!

Sancia picks up another magazine.

My mother is obsessed with this idea that I have an eating disorder, so she's always leaving magazines like this lying around 'accidentally on purpose'.

What's this? 'TEN TELL-TALE SIGNS THAT YOU HAVE AN EATING DISORDER'. Well, let's just have a look at this shall we?

1. SEVERE WEIGHT LOSS
Look, I just have this incredibly fast metabolism... I eat heaps, as much as I like, more than most people. I just burn off heaps when I'm under stress. I was overweight anyway, so it's not like it was severe. Some people are genetically thin. Look at the supermodels... they just totally pig out. In last month's Vogue, I saw Kate Moss eating a biscuit, I am not lying. I didn't even think about my weight... it just fell off.

2. CHANGES IN THE PATTERN OF MEALTIMES
It's just a Western concept anyway, the idea that we all eat together like a herd of cows. Look, I'm just one of those people who doesn't

eat breakfast, and I'm always so busy at lunchtime, I forget to eat... and you get really bad nightmares if you eat late at night. Jane Fonda says: 'Always go to bed hungry' and how much money does she make? As all the eastern philosophers say: 'Follow your instincts'. And mine just tell me to eat a lot of lettuce and drink diet coke.

3. OBSESSIVE PREPARATION OF FOOD
I just love to cook... that should tell you something. I love being around food. And you know how it is when you cook, often you just aren't hungry when the meal is on the table. But I do love to watch people eat. It's part of life.
I don't like anyone else to prepare my food for me... it's a ritual thing and I just want to make sure there aren't any toxins in my body.

4. IRRATIONAL AMOUNTS OF EXERCISE
I am a really uptight person and if I don't exercise I just get really batty. Besides if you don't exercise, you just end up getting osteoporosis. Everyone knows that. Demi Moore and those guys spend seven hours in the gym... you could say that's irrational but they are hardly anorexic. Look at Carl Lewis... would you say he was anorexic?
I think the person who wrote this article could be irrational.

5. CONSTANT CHEWING OF GUM
I read somewhere that John Lennon chewed six packs a day... so I suppose he's anorexic as well? Besides, chewing gum is loaded with sugar... so that just proves I don't have a problem with my weight.

6. PICKING FROM THE FRIDGE
What's wrong with that? But little brother does it. I just like to taste food. So right... now you're saying you don't want me to eat. This is stupid.

7. BAD BREATH
What, am I perfect?

8. LAXATIVE ABUSE
My grandma takes laxatives. Are we going to haul her off to hospital, are we?

Sometimes I have trouble going to the toilet... lots of people do. I suppose if I had lots of money I could go and have a colonic flush every day—that's where they flush out your bowels with water—how gross is that?

9. IRREGULAR OR NON EXISTENT MENSTRUATION
My period was never regular... and lots of people lose their periods under stress. I hate these articles... I mean, what's regular anyway? This person should define their terms.

10. CHANGES IN BEHAVIOUR
Oh, right. Let's take everyone in the whole world off to hospital then.

Anyway I'm just growing up and don't like doing the things I used to do. Sometimes I'm happy, sometimes I'm sad. I suppose I could always have a lobotomy.

I just focus on different things at different times... I've always been like that. I'm just private. I don't like the whole world knowing everything about me.

And I especially don't like people walking around with dumb magazine articles like this and spying on me and watching everything I do.

There is nothing wrong with me, it's just a stage I'm going through.
The only problem with me is that I'm too fat.

So get off my case... leave me alone!

IN THE MIRROR

Sancia poses in the mirror... she discovers her hair is falling out, her teeth are rotting, her skin transparent and a light fur is growing on her arms and face.

She is extremely weak and wearily climbs into her bed.

HOSPITAL

Uh Oh...

I've really done it this time. I'm in hospital.

The embarrassing thing is... there's nothing wrong with me.
Well, nothing that a sausage roll wouldn't fix.
If I could eat a sausage roll.
If I could eat anything.
But I can't.

Mum's bought me a new nightie.
I don't need a new nightie.
The girls will come and visit me sitting up in bed in my new nightie.
They'll bring flowers and cards... they won't bring a box of chocolates.

'Don't be stupid... she won't eat chocolates. They're fattening... she won't eat anything fattening, der brain. Anyway she's really sick. Buy her something she'll like. Buy her twenty packets of chewy.'

What will they think when they find out it's only anorexia nervosa.
They'll hate me.
I wish I had cancer of something.
Or a tumour.
Maybe a hole in the heart.

I must have a hole in the heart

To make everyone worry like this.
I'm going to put on weight just lying here.
They want to keep me here to fatten me up
Like a battery pig.

I hate being here
I want to go home.
Oh no.
Visitors...

Hello everyone.

Lovely to see you.
Great, I feel fine... I'm just a little bit tired.
They're doing some tests in the morning.
Thanks for the juicy fruit.
But I can't eat after 8 pm.
Not that that will be a problem.
Ha ha ha.

I can't believe I actually laughed
Right in their faces.
They were all sitting here with sad faces
And I laughed.
I wish I could die.

So, Doc... how am I doing?
Hair falling out
Scaly skin
Loose teeth
Slow pulse
Hypoglycaemia
Periods stopped
Tooth enamel wearing off
Fungus in the fingernails
Dehydration
Constipation
Malnutrition
And I have fur growing on my body...
Yeah... but apart from that...
How am I?

I've got IT
IT's official.
Anorexia Nervosa.
Now everyone will know.

Did you hear?
Sancia is in hospital because she won't eat her tea.

And it's lovely rice pudding for dinner again.

Oh God...
If only...
If only I could be...
Five stone.

AT THE PSYCHIATRIST'S OFFICE

Now five stone seemed like a good idea to me... but my parents had other ideas. So instead of letting me do something useful like go for a jog... or go on a fruit juice fast... they sent me to a psychiatrist... a head doctor for the mentally ill, the emotionally handicapped.

Which was bizarre... I hadn't lost my mind... just my appetite.

Sancia sits in a chair for 'consultation'.

Oh yes, I'm really glad to be back at school. And I'm pleased with the weight I've put on. I really want to eat more and yes... eight and a half stone seems like a good idea.

Why not nine stone... why not 15 stone... hey, why stop there, why not 25 stone? Let's all enjoy watching me grow into an enormous fat whale... a pile of blubber as big as a block of flats.

Oh yes. I very much enjoy sharing my feelings here every week.
I am feeling enabled.
And very empowered.
My inner child... ?

How could I tell him my inner child didn't want dinner either.

There's just one thing... This isn't important... it's just a little thing... but I thought I should mention it.
I'm sort of starting to bring my food up a little bit. Just vomiting a little bit... now and then.

Oh yeah, I'm still eating heaps.
Oh... then it's not a worry... as long as some of it stays down.

The most important thing is that I eat.

YES.

I don't think he realised quite what he had said 'yes' to, because after years of keeping my hunger under control, finally...
The Beast Was Loose.
Be Afraid, Be Very, Very Afraid!

'BINGEING WITH SANCIA'

On a TV studio set.

'Thanks Bert... '

HELLO AND WELCOME to 'Bingeing With Sancia', a favourite segment of ours here on 'What is the Matter with Mary Jane?', our Anorexia-Bulimia lifestyle program.

Of course binge eating is becoming more and more popular these days. We've all heard of celebrity bulimics... Jane Fonda, Elton John, Sally Field, Billy Jean King and what with the ever glamorous Princess Diana admitting to being 'bulimic'... it does look like a quick and easy answer to that figure you've always wanted. But is it? There's a whole lot more to it than fingers down the throat, a quick little vomit and then slip into those size eight jeans, believe me!

Many folk have asked me: 'Sancia, how do I go about bingeing? Is it difficult, is it expensive, what do I wear?

So today we're going to look at a classic binge.
Firstly, do set aside an evening by yourself, no TV, telephone off the hook and no music to distract you (unless you have K-Tel's 'Music to Vomit By'... a compilation of Billy Ray Cyrus and Michael Bolton tracks), oh and you'll need about $25 to $30.

If you can wear something you don't mind getting stained... that's great. But be prepared to ruin your best clothes... remembering that bingeing can strike at any time.

You wonder how the rich and famous manage in those gorgeous frocks, don't you? Well, at least they don't have to queue for the ladies.

I know you're thinking... what about those tell tale bits of food left floating in the bowl? Perhaps that's why a celebrity always carries a handbag.

A word of warning girls... cocktail hats with netting veils are probably NOT a good idea.

OK? Great!

Now we all know how it starts... it's 4 pm, you've hardly eaten a thing all day, your tummy is roaring and you think: 'Hmm, perhaps I'll eat an apple' but, no, before you've realised, you're in the pastry shop and whoa, we're off.

She takes a shopping basket to the fridge.

OK, firstly in the pastry shop we're looking for your basic carbohydrates... you want to grab about six cakes... perhaps three iced cream buns and a few cream cakes... maybe some sausage rolls.

Find a quiet spot... behind the shop is a good place... and just shovel these down as fast as you can...

She shoves the food into a food blender.

Let's push the gluggy, doughy ones down first, without having a drink if you can, and of course don't bother about chewing because we want them to come up in a good solid lump when we get home.

There we go... let's leave that for a moment.

Now, holding our tummies in tightly, it's off to the supermarket.

She returns to the fridge.

We all know it's important to buy the best ingredients we can afford, so today we're looking for sure fire throw up material... anything soft and sweet.

Stay away from anything spicy or crunchy because the last thing we want here is to rip our throats out as it comes up.

So, I have here soft bread rolls, jam, Mint slices, Tim Tams (a family favourite... but the kids won't be getting their hands on these), cake, raisin bread, chocolate or caramel topping, custard, sugar, cornflakes (hello to our lovely sponsors at Kelloggs), milk, Milo (always looking to buy Australian made of course) cheesecake, icing, honey, peanut butter, ice cream and, of course, good old Golden Syrup.

What about chocolate? You're thinking. Be very careful about chocolate... it does tend to decompose rapidly and stay in the stomach where it can be absorbed and turn into dreaded FAT.

Grab everything as fast as you can... into the trolley they go... [*Sancia returns to the table.*] You can certainly feel free to finish off your pastries, donuts or packets of Cheezels [*added to blender*] or what have you, as you race through the aisles. If you're feeling a little thirsty, I would recommend apricot nectar [*added to blender*] to wash the food down... From my experience its smooth and sweet consistency makes it an ideal vomiting aid. OK? Great!

So, with everything in the car, it's time to head for home. Now time is important here, because who knows how many calories we are absorbing through the stomach lining, the throat, maybe even the cheeks as we keep the food in our bodies.

Oh, did I mention the barbecued chickens? I usually grab a couple, with stuffing, and start on them in the car...

She adds bits of chicken to the blender.

Do be careful here... driving with a huge bloated stomach, packets of food opened all over the seats and hands covered in chicken fat is definitely a traffic hazard.

In the event of an accident try explaining exactly what you are doing to a policeman you've just thrown up all over!
And darlings, if the phone rings... forget it!

Once home, grab the food, run inside and head for the toilet.

Now I should explain my method... I'm a regurgitator... by that I mean that I don't use my fingers to vomit.
I didn't have to train myself, I found that because I'm so tense when I

eat, and hold my stomach so tightly, the food just rises of its own accord.

OK? Great!

And, in the toilet...

> *She pours the contents of the blender into the toilet.*

...the first part of our binge is a huge success... a big mass... you can see the chocolate, which is a relief, we don't want that staying down. Actually you might like to use the kitchen tongs to have a good poke around to identify all the various ingredients.

Can you get a close up of that, camera three?

Now we come to the most enjoyable part of the binge... eating in peace and quiet.

Take your ingredients into the kitchen and breathing steadily, feeling a little light headed, begin picking at a pastry until you pick up speed... [*Putting the items into the blender.*] Cheezels, Tim Tams, ice cream... swallow the lot, then to the toilet again.

> *She pours the contents into the toilet.*

This should come up easily... and produce a severe headache and throbbing in the temples.

In the kitchen again, with a sausage roll in one hand while preparing a huge bowl of cornflakes, milk and sugar... [*Into the blender.*] down it goes and then off to the toilet. [*Into toilet.*]

Up it comes again... your eyes should really be aching now.

You should be feeling extremely tired and dizzy now as you finish the ice cream covered in Milo, followed by the Tim Tams and Mint slices, then off to the toilet to vomit once more.

Our head is aching, our eyes are swollen and sore, the throat and mouth feeling red raw, we can't stop now... stuffing in the rest of the chicken and drinking a bottle of chocolate topping until we are off to the toilet to throw up again.

The chocolate is dangerous, it hasn't come up, so if this happens drink water until you throw up and throw up until you can only see bile in the toilet bowl.

Now just sit on the toilet and breathe deeply, aware of the sore muscles in your stomach, the burping acidic taste, scratchy, furry teeth, dry face and staring eyes. Just take a drink of water, sit and recover.

Feel your swollen tongue and eyes protruding.

Now get the food out again and repeat the process. You're exhausted, push the food down.
Finish the chicken carcass, throw up.
Toast, jam and ice cream, throw up again.
Throw up cornflakes, custard and sugar,
Throw up Cheezels and chocolate,
Throw up water.

> *She goes back to toilet.*

And throw and throw and throw and throw and throw...
Throw, throw, throw, throw until you are sweating, your gut is aching, your mouth bloated, ears and eyes sore, your back muscles strained and ripped, until you are on the point of passing out.

Lie on the bathroom floor until the dizziness passes.
Close your eyes, breathe deeply and evenly and repeat: 'I am a fat, selfish pig. I am a loser, coward, I am ugly, a waste of space.'

That's all for 'Bingeing With Sancia'... see you same time tomorrow... and the next day... and the next day after that!

AFTER THE BINGE

Well... this is a fine mess you've gotten us both into.

You'd better clean this up, you ugly, disgusting pig. Have a good look at yourself... your skin's wrecked, your face is bloated! You've put on weight.
Everybody hates you because you're so sly.
I wouldn't want to be in your shoes.

I know, I know... but what am I going to do?

You could do some exercise... go to the gym.

No... I can't... I can't do this any more...

Oh, so you want to be seven and a half stone...

No... no... I don't, but I just want this to end.

Mum?
Mum is that you?
I'm not doing anything.
No... don't come in.
No... I don't want you to come in.
I'm not here.
There's nobody here.
There's nobody here.

...

It was then that I realised that I probably had a problem.

After being bulimic on and off for ten years... one day I almost choked on some half regurgitated food...

Not a very glamorous end for Princess Sancia... no crystal casket, no woodland clearing strewn with rose petals... just dead on the toilet floor in a pool of her own vomit.

Cough, cough, cough.

Up came a piece of poisoned apple.

And after 16 years of silence... locked in a dark tower... I finally opened my mouth.

Of course I had opened my mouth to throw up food.
And as an actress I had opened my mouth to speak words others had written... thousands of them, torrents of words.
And I had opened my mouth to whisper words of hate to myself.
And I had opened my mouth to lie to others.

But I had never opened my mouth to tell the truth.
And the first word that came out of my mouth? HELP.

So I looked for help. And after a couple of years followed by false starts, near rescues and blind alleys, six months ago I saw an eating disorder specialist... the person I should have seen when I was 16.

'Oh my God Sancia... you are so thin... You are smaller than Heather Locklear... you must be a size zero. I reckon you should see an eating disorder specialist.'

And we stopped talking about food and my weight and started to talk about my mind and my soul.

So why me? Why Anorexia?

I wish I could say it was because of my mother's unreasonable hopes that I would become a beautiful, accomplished woman.
I wish I could say it was because my father called me 'Butch'.
Or that my brother called me 'Moon Face'.
I wish I could say it was because of Barbie or the Brady Bunch... Or Nicole Trewicke... a model in Dolly magazine whose thighs never met in the middle.
And of course I'd love to say it was all my fault.

But you might as well ask me why my voice sounds the way it does.

Why I walk the way I do. Or why I dream what I dream. Because Anorexia Nervosa is a psychiatric illness... a small, quiet, submissive madness... and what is it in this life which sends us quietly mad?

Right now, for me it feels so hard to imagine a life without Anorexia... the only thing I'm certain of is that I have no life with Anorexia.

And so my life continues... one meal at a time.

IN THE MIRROR

Sancia looks in the mirror and finds some acceptance there.

She walks off stage.

A STUDY GUIDE
For Teachers and Students

Written by
Dianne Mackenzie
Curriculum Officer for English and Drama, NSW
&
Henrietta Stathopoulos, MA (Comms) Dip. Ed.
Senior Drama/English teacher

What is the Matter with Mary Jane? is Sancia Robinson's story – a story about a recovering anorexic and bulimic. To stand in front of an audience sharing such a traumatic period in her life, having fought the diseases for over fourteen years, obviously takes great courage in a performer.

A graduate of NIDA, Sancia has numerous theatre, television, and film credits to her name, including *Harp in the South* (STC), *The Tempest* (MTC), *Abingdon Square* (Belvoir Street), *Blue Heelers*, *A Country Practice*, and *Voices*.

The monodrama *What is the Matter with Mary Jane?* takes its audience into the painful reality of a woman afflicted by eating disorders and shows how the realisation that her condition was an illness meant that she could begin the slow process of recovery.

Robinson's impressive list of achievements in the competitive world of the theatre makes it hard to believe that she has suffered from such a crippling condition. Yet, in another way, the importance of physical image and the gratification of audience approval which forms part of every actor's consciousness, connect with the manifestation of this kind of illness in a very obvious way.

What is the Matter with Mary Jane? provided Sancia Robinson with a way of 'coming out'. In honestly portraying the torturous journey of her young life, she has hoped to reach out to young people who may be in danger of travelling the same road. There is also an element of therapeutic release involved in the act of exposing the truth about herself. Society's obsession with body image can lead to self-hatred and the experiences portrayed in this play have more than a personal significance. In the play, Sancia presents a documentation of the process of the disease and the hope of a liberation which may help others to deal with this problem, and to survive it.

   Like most anorexics/bulimics, Sancia developed an obsession with her weight in her mid-teens, a vulnerable time for many victims. Her vulnerability and low self-esteem continued to plague her into her 30s. Sancia Robinson has experienced all the phases of her illness, the withdrawal from society, the physical debilitation, the over-use of physical exercise. She tried many solutions and finally, working with a therapist who specialises in eating disorders, Sancia Robinson managed to overcome the illness. She says of it, however, that like many forms of addiction, anorexia/bulimia is a disease that must be confronted over and over again, 'one meal at a time'. In this play, with the help of her friend Wendy Harmer, she tackles the subject in a humorous way making it accessible to audiences of any kind.

WENDY HARMER

There can be no doubt that Wendy Harmer is a talented individual. Her career as the leading female comedian in Australia has ranged from live performances as a stand-up comic, to compering ABC's *The Big Gig*, the cut and thrust of *World Series Debating*, and waking up Sydney radio listeners on 2-DAY FM. Her wit continues to entertain readers of various magazine columns including the *Sydney Morning Herald*'s 'Good Weekend'. In *What is the Matter with Mary Jane?*, Harmer assumed the roles of both playwright and director.

   Harmer (*née* Brown) was born in country Victoria, the eldest of four children. Her father was a country schoolteacher and the family moved often, the children having to change schools and make new friends each time. Harmer's position was made more difficult since she was born with a cleft palate and lip. The attitude of children to those who are 'different' in any way, is not always welcoming and Harmer learnt to use her wits to establish herself. Her perception of the destructiveness of society's fascination with body image, one of the significant issues in this play, is easy to understand.

Her working career started as a journalist in Geelong, but she eventually gave up journalism and the comparative security of reporting on local government events for the chaotic, and sometimes rewarding, world of comedy.

Having performed in, and written for, ABC TV's *The Gillies Report* and *The Big Gig*, Harmer became one of Australia's top female comedians. She has been a regular performer on comedy circuits here and overseas during the past fifteen years, as well as adding numerous writing credits to her name including *Backstage Pass*, a play for adolescents, *Love Gone Wrong*, a novel about the trials and tribulations of relationships, and *It's a Joke, Joyce*, a history of Australian female comedy.

During the boom in Australian comedy that occurred the 1980s, Wendy Harmer was one of the few to broaden the content of her humour, which, like that of many female performers at the time, was greatly influenced by Feminism. Yet she continues to challenge her audiences to think about the kaleidoscope of things which effect our lives from Barbie dolls to love, from the idiosyncrasies of our public figures to Sunday driving with Dad..

Like Sancia Robinson, Harmer herself has had to deal with her own 'self-conscious pain'. She too experienced the effects of rejection because of the irregularity of her facial features. It was her father who helped her deal with life and its harsh cruelties, preventing her from withdrawing, encouraging her to read the paper aloud to visitors. Harsh and confronting lessons.

Comedy too can be confronting, as *What is the Matter with Mary Jane?* proves. Through Sancia Robinson's sometimes frightening and sometimes funny story, Harmer presents us with an extraordinary theatrical experience. The subject of Anorexia and Bulimia is hardly humorous, yet Harmer believed that Sancia's story – the struggle of a close friend suffering from these disorders – needed to be presented.

FORM AND STYLE

In choosing the form of monodrama, to be performed by the actor whose story the play tells, Wendy Harmer ensured a special intimacy was added to the experience of *What is the Matter with Mary Jane?*

Monodrama has been a particular feature of Australian Theatre since the work of the New Wave Dramatists of the 1970s: Jack Hibberd's *A Stretch of the Imagination* (1972), Ron Blair's *The Christian Brothers* (1975), and Steve J. Spear's *The Elocution of Benjamin Franklin* (1976) and Barry Dickin's *Lennie Lower* (1982) being notable early examples. These were all plays written by males for male performers, often portraying the individual struggling against and alienated from the mainstream. Monodramas for women performers were also written; Barry Dickin's *Bridal Suite* (1979) and *The Death of Minnie* (1980) for example. With the development of Women's Theatre following the Women's Movement, in the 1980s monodrama became a popular form. Used by playwrights such as Beverley Dunn in *To Botany Bay in a Bondi Tram* (1984), the characters presented tended to be more multifaceted and they often carried a more positive and affirming message. The work of Robyn Archer in cabaret-style musical monodrama in performances such as *A Star is Torn* demonstrated the broad possibilities of this genre.

In the monodrama a complete theatrical work is performed by one actor who portrays either a single character, or multiple characters in the dramatic situation. The demands on the actor in such a performance are great, both physically and emotionally. Through the actor's performance skills, not only his or her own role, but the roles of other characters with whom the protagonist interacts (no matter how fleetingly) must be brought to life for the audience. While other theatrical elements such as lighting and design, may help create veracity and changes of mood and pace as well as emotional intensity, in no other genre does so much depend on the single actor, who must work without the collaborative support and dynamic interaction with other actors which aids performance in other plays.

Monodramas can easily suffer from a narrowing of focus and a lack of variety in the range of experience which they portray. In the best monodramas, however, the audience is offered an intensity of focus and a special intimacy with character. The actor speaks directly to the audience for the whole performance.

The use of the individual voice of the character, not only necessarily engages the audience in a very direct relationship to the character, but allows the character to speak more potently with their individual voice, of experiences, thoughts and feelings.

Wendy Harmer has used the genre to great effect in *What is the Matter with Mary Jane?* Since the play is concerned with a particular individual's struggle with a very personal 'madness' – anorexia/bulimia – the intense focus provided by the genre is most appropriate to the revelation of the personal anguish and horrors of the struggle to survive.

Through the use of the device of the audience as 'the mirror', a powerful involvement of the audience is created. Yet the danger that the personal nature of the struggle portrayed in this play might lead to an oppressively maudlin process is prevented by the clever manipulation of language, pace of performance, imaginative recreation of place and situation, and most significantly by the objectifying use of humour. While the confessional intensity of this play might have been overwhelming since the performer was herself the subject of its exploration, the explicit humour of the piece prevents this from being the case. The courage with which the subject of the text, played out by the actor whose life experience is being 'actually' enacted, is reinforced by the humour with which the actor/subject (Sancia), can stand back from the experience and describe its process. Though the style of the play appears to be naturalistic, this is a very Brechtian device, which provides an essential safety measure for performer and audience. In the famous Brechtian acting experience, actors are required to 'describe' an incident as witnesses, rather than to 'enact' it as participants. Here the actor is witness to her very own personal trauma and the distancing of the Brechtian technique is essential to the audience capturing that anguished experience in an appropriate context.

Sancia Robinson herself sees the play as having been a therapeutic experience:

> Who would have thought that a week ago I couldn't even talk about this?' she said. 'It's been really liberating to see anorexia as an illness, because I feel if it's an illness then I can recover from it.
>
> *Daily Telegraph-Mirror,* 27/2/95

However, the play has a more general significance for its audiences. The first performances took place at the Wharf Theatre in 1995 as part of the ICI/Sydney Theatre Company's Education Program, aimed at school student audiences. As a Theatre in Education (TIE) piece, the play attempts to explore an issue which affects young people, and young women in particular – the widespread phenomena of the eating disorders, anorexia and bulimia. TIE performances have undergone many changes since the early productions where a naturalistic style combined with a directly didactic content, related to either curriculum issues or adolescent problems, predominated. Lack of funding, financial constraints limiting the number of actors involved, and the need to use flexible, simple staging techniques were also powerful considerations affecting the styles adopted by TIE productions. There has been an accepted critical opinion amongst many in the theatre community that in being conscientiously didactic many TIE performances for young people destroyed the essence of a 'theatrical experience' for their audiences. Yet TIE and performances for young people have continued, despite criticism, to be a vital form of theatre.

What is the Matter with Mary Jane? reflects some of these TIE characteristics. The use of the genre of monodrama automatically solves the problem of cast size, and the use of minimal staging effects makes the performance of the play viable in a range of venues. The language, humour, and style of the play also appeal to the context of current youth culture. The play certainly has a powerful and urgent message for youth, yet in exploring the experiences of one young woman, it avoids the tendency to lecture to its audience by providing an exciting and intelligent theatrical experience.

STRUCTURE

What is the Matter with Mary Jane? is divided into eleven segments, each of which provides the audience with some insight into the obsessive behaviour displayed by the victims of eating disorders and the self-hatred which drives them.

1. INTRODUCTION (PAGE 9)

The play begins with the actor on stage looking at herself in the mirror, squeezing her facial pimples. The audience itself is the mirror, and witness to the embarrassment felt by the character who recognises the audience's presence and directly addresses herself to them. And so we are drawn, through the looking glass, into a world no less bizarre than that of Alice in her Wonderland.

The use of the mirror is central to the concerns of the play. Mirrors reflect, show us an image of ourselves. Mirrors also distort. Yet no matter how inaccurate their reflection may be, the real distortion of what we think we see in the mirror is produced by our own minds.

The Sancia we are introduced to is the one who is '16 years old' and 'size 10' though she thinks she should be 'size 8'. The Sancia introducing this earlier self is an adult – and she is *still* size 10. After telling the audience her name and age, what she relates about herself is how she looks – or rather how she thinks *they* think she looks: 'I know you are looking at me thinking "Boy, what a fat pig ... she sure could lose a few kilos."'

This early comment reveals so much of the nature of the psychological reality experienced by those who suffer from eating disorders: a sense of separation from others, an objectification of the self as a body needing to be controlled, and a distorted interpretation of the image which is seen in the gaze of others. The self-hatred of the anorexic is captured in the frequent comparisons of the body with images of food. Her body is a 'bratwurst sausage and a battered saveloy'. The language explodes with alliteration and assonance: she has a 'bean bag bum, a whopping big bag of Cheezels inside [her] jeans'. From bum to stomach the chant proceeds: 'paunchy, pudgy, roly poly, tubby gut – spud gut, old blubber belly. Bag of jelly bean belly'. The images build up as a ritual litany in which the self really is what it eats. The whole body is seen in images of food: Arms are 'chiko rolls', she has 'fish fingers' and 'potato wedge legs'; the whole body is a 'bag of junk' with 'the brain of a chicken nugget'. The association of fat and rubbish with the junk foods which form so great an element in the adolescent diet culminates with a parody of the famous jingle:

Two all beef legs
No neck
Huge boobs
Fat cheeks
All on a sesame seed bum.

The idea of attaining the perfect image, symbolised by achievement in a beauty contest is introduced as part of this litany of self-abuse: 'Miss Biscuit Barrel. Miss Monte Carlo', and that famous icon of the anorexic,

Princess Diana, is invoked: 'Princess Chocolate Royal'. So involved in this ritual of self-flagellation is the character, that she self-consciously must bring herself back to the reality of the audience and away from her self-absorption with her body with: 'I'm sorry... what did you say your name was again?', to tell them that she is really Sancia Robinson – aged thirty, and still a size ten.

The development of a distorted world of fantasy is also characteristic of this 'disease', and the image of the Fairy Princess is introduced in the first segment, along with another twisted advertising slogan promising transformation, 'It won't happen overnight, but it will happen'. The reality of the lives of the fairy story princesses is quite other than the fables of childhood. The fairy-story princesses of today – the models, actors, royal icons – are tortured beauties, 'angst ridden, refusing food... locked in towers.' A powerful and disturbing truth is expressed here. In fairy tales too, princesses don't eat since 'even the apples are poisoned'. Yet the reality is that to accept being human, we have to acknowledge that fairy tales are not written about 'plump post-adolescent princesses.' In the world of modern fable, the world of advertising, image and the Romance Novel, this is not the material from which the gold of glamour is spun.

The struggle to accept the reality of limitation and ordinariness is part of every journey to wholeness and maturity. The temptation to escape that acceptance can lead to disaster and this is essentially what this play articulates. As Sancia explains:

> I could see I was in danger of turning into a fairly ordinary common fat frog. And if I couldn't control the rest of my life... there was one Magic Kingdom of which I was sole ruler... my body.

In these words, Harmer reveals the link between anorexia and the adolescent's need to forge an identity. The issue is one of control, of being in control of one's destiny through a distorted manipulation of the self – conceived as, or represented in, one's very body – that 'too, too, solid flesh...' which the purveyors of the diet and slimming industry, (savagely sent up here in the play) promise to 'melt' so painlessly for us.

Sancia, the expert on calorie content, not only gains a sense of control but also approbation and attention from her peers for:

> My mother and father were always telling me what to do.
> Nobody noticed me at school.
> I had no life of my own.
> I was just ordinary.
> And then I lost weight.
> Now I'm the size of a pea and life is wonderful.

2. IN THE MIRROR (PAGE 13)
The second segment is written in four line stanzas which can be delivered like an advertising jingle but which parody the poetry of childhood. The verse explores the nature of adolescent dreams: being 'cool', pictured in magazines, driving fast cars, escorted by the icons of female desire, being popular – being a 'star'. A world in which dieting promises to be 'a miracle cure for everything that's wrong in your miserable little life.'

3. AT THE TABLE (PAGE 15)
Segment three grounds the play back in reality. It begins with a ritualistic intonation of the caloric content of foods that leads into a conversation between the adolescent Sancia and her mother. Though mother is not seen on the stage, the struggle of wills between the two is realistically delineated in the monologue which captures Sancia's internal responses to the mother's remarks. The mother's attempts to persuade her daughter to eat, see her cast in the role of the enemy; someone to do battle with; to manipulate and use as the rationalised cause of the daughter's illness. Mother deserves to be punished: 'No, I don't want anything else. (That'll teach her.)' Adult members of the audience with adolescent children will find the situation and the manufactured tantrum

a familiar experience! 'See what she's doing to me ? She wants me to be fat and ugly.'

4. JOGGING (PAGE 17)

This segment begins with more self-abuse – 'You are a pig...sitting up to the trough with your little trotters on the table...' – and the words segue the action into the next aspect of anorexia which Harmer wishes to explore, the excessive over-use of exercise to lose weight as the actor jogs herself into exhaustion. The body of the anorexic becomes the betrayer in this sequence, to be taken in charge by the mind: 'From now on you are under arrest and will be punished.' The image expresses aptly a sense of the split in the identity of the anorexic between mind and body and is reinforced in the macabre conversation with the self which concludes the segment:

> Hang on a minute... who are you?
> You, of course.
> Where are we going?
> Six stone.

5. EXCUSES (PAGE 18)

This is a particularly amusing section of the play that heralds an easing of tempo with an amazingly versatile and complete list of excuses used by the character to avoid situations in which she might be expected to eat. The list ranges from being allergic or having diabetes to 'engaging in a political boycott.' Behind the humour, starkly underlining the procession of negative responses to invitations to life, is the terrifying fact that gradually the anorexic ceases to be involved in all the normal social interactions with other people. She cancels dates and entertainments and loses friends. The telephone, used here as both the literal and symbolic link to the world outside the Self, ceases to ring. And despite the recognition that 'everyone thinks you're weird', the struggle for control continues. The pathos of the last question changes the mood again and prepares the audience for the grotesque seriousness of the segments which follow:

> But when will I be allowed to stop all this?
> When you're perfect.

6. IN THE TOILET (PAGE 21)
Sancia, enjoying 'a good night in', swallows Laxettes and spends her time reading Supermodel magazines on the toilet. This segment attempts to convey information about the symptoms which can be observed in anorexics and to explore the effects of the myths of the 'super-creatures' (models, etc.) who seem so divorced from ordinary mortals that they must have arrived 'as small children from another planet'.

In this section, the manner in which the underlying message is conveyed to the audience is not quite as effective as in other sections of the play. Sancia's reading out of a long list of 'Tell-tale Signs of Eating Disorders' is in danger of dwindling into a lecture and lacks the dramatic effectiveness of scenes in which the situation and action communicate the ideas theatrically. The seriousness of the psychological dimensions of the 'disease' is captured by the irony of some of Sancia's reactions to the magazine article's descriptions of symptoms such as secretive changes in behaviour: 'I don't like the whole world knowing everything about me... spying on me and watching everything I do.'

7. IN THE MIRROR (PAGE 26)
This segment moves the play on towards confronting the increasingly serious nature of her condition. In the mirror Sancia discovers her hair is falling out, her teeth are rotting and she climbs into bed to introduce the next two sections which are set at a hospital and the psychiatrist's office.

8. HOSPITAL (PAGE 27)
In this segment Harmer uses the language of youth culture to reflect the

reaction of Sancia's friends to her illness '... she won't eat anything fattening, der brain'. The litany of the effects of her now officially diagnosed anorexia continues: 'Dehydration/Constipation/Malnutrition', and still she desires to be even slimmer. 'If only I could be... five stone...' With each phase of her progressive decline, charted through each segment, her slimming goals become yet more extreme.

9. AT THE PSYCHIATRIST'S OFFICE (PAGE 29)

Denial of the illness continues even when faced with psychiatric care. 'I hadn't lost my mind... just my appetite.' The manipulative anorexic can even cleverly parrot the language of therapy – 'I am feeling enabled... very empowered... my inner child' – and finally uses the psychiatric advice that it is alright to be 'just vomiting a little bit ...' to justify her compulsive behaviour – so setting loose 'The Beast' of Bulimia.

10. BINGEING WITH SANCIA (PAGE 30)

The climax of the play is reached in this segment which parodies the ubiquitous television health/lifestyle shows. The 'exercise' demonstrated here is a how-to-do-it blueprint for the art of bingeing. The humour is extremely savage, carried out to 'K-Tel's Music to Vomit By'. Gross details of the bulimic condition are launched at the audience as Sancia describes the bulimic rich and famous leaving 'tell-tale bits of food... floating in the bowl/ Perhaps that's why a celebrity always carries a handbag.'

In the frenzy to consume, Sancia uses a blender to 'push the gluggy, doughy ones down first'. The satire of her knowledgeable advice to avoid solid foods 'because the last thing we want here is to rip our throats out as it comes up' is typical of the painfully black humour of this segment. When the binge is over, rather like the exhaustion after a good workout, the bulimic rests with an exhausted stomach, a dry, tight face, staring eyes, and 'swollen tongue and eyes pounding'. The process is then repeated, in a horrifying ritual, building to a climax – 'and throw and throw and throw and throw' – during which Sancia intones the self-abusive mantra: 'I am a fat selfish pig. I am a loser, coward. I am ugly, a waste of space.'

11. AFTER THE BINGE (PAGE 36)

The climax of the binge is followed by a change of pace, though the self-reflective humour continues with a line from Laurel and Hardy – 'a fine mess you've gotten us both into'. The words again summon the spectre of a divided self. The pathos of her cry for help is at the same time a denial: 'I'm not here./There's nobody here./There's nobody here.'

Sancia reveals that after ten years of this agony only the threat of death made her confront the problem as 'one day I almost choked on some half-regurgitated food...'

There is a return to the imagery of the fairy princess at the beginning of the play. She has undergone '16 years of silence... locked in a dark tower'. For Princess Sancia there could be 'no crystal casket, no woodland clearing strewn with rose petals... just dead on the toilet floor in a pool of her own vomit.'

The play finally offers no real answer to the question of why this illness, this 'small, quiet, submissive madness' afflicts her. Or, indeed, to what it is 'in this life which sends us quietly mad'. The questions could be aimed at many compulsive and disturbed behaviours.

In looking beyond the symptoms of the disease, with professional help, Sancia has 'stopped talking about food and my weight and started to talk about my mind and my soul.' Through this daily process of facing her real self has come the glimmer of hope for a liberation which must be struggled for as 'life continues... one meal at a time.'

In the closing moment of the play, Sancia gazes in 'the mirror' and finds 'some acceptance there'. The duality of her role as secret anorexic and public actress finding approval in the applause of an audience, is startlingly embodied in this last moment.

ISSUES

This monodrama, while it has its essential focus on the experience of anorexia and bulimia, inevitably touches on a number of issues related to that experience.

The audience certainly learns a great deal about the particular manifestations of the disease. We see Sancia's ingenious attempts to hide her condition from others, especially in the section called 'Excuses'. 'At the Table' neatly sketches the conflict both within and between herself and her mother. 'Jogging' shows the audience an anorexic using excessive exercise in a frenzy of self-abuse. 'In the Toilet' and 'Bingeing with Sancia' bring the horrors of bulimia into sharp focus. The manipulations of the anorexic/bulimic are demonstrated throughout the play but they are brought specifically to the fore in one of the last sections, 'Hospital'.

Overall, the performance attempts to educate its audience to recognise the symptoms and effects of eating disorders not by preaching, but by inviting the audience into the world of a victim of the disease.

In the opening segments, Harmer introduces the idea of the influence of the images created by the fairy stories and the myths of childhood. Snow White and the poisoned apple – an image of food which if consumed, brings destruction – is particularly apt for Harmer's purposes. The idea, planted in little girls' minds, that fairy princesses remain, like the Lady of Shallot, locked safely in their towers, aloof from the mess of ordinary life where one is likely to become an 'ordinary common fat frog' is returned to at the end of the play when Sancia realises that she has spent her life silently 'locked in a dark tower' from which she must now break free. The play itself is a public step outside, into the 'real' world through the protective fantasy of theatre.

The 'beauty myth' and the attainment of the perfect physical image are, as the play points out so forcefully, fabricated by the media and reinforced by the creation of icons of success. These icons, from Princess Diana to supermodels like Elle Macpherson and actors and pop stars, are created as glittering symbols of how women must be if they desire to be valued. Thinness, not cleanliness, in our society, is next to Godliness. The Calvinists of the Reformation were convinced that being the elect of the Lord was demonstrated in one's worldly success and accumulation of wealth – such was the Reformists' belief in the interface between religion and the rise of capitalism. In modern Western society, the media preaches and seduces us with the doctrine of 'you can be and have it all'. Every day, glossy magazines, television, advertising, film, and newspapers, show that it is the thin and (therefore) beautiful who shall inherit the earth and all its goodies. As night follows day, so success, money, chic clothes, fast cars, and glamorous partners will follow the achievement of a virtuously skinny body.

The overwhelming need to be accepted, that shapes so much adolescent behaviour, is another element in Harmer's examination of the multifaceted causes of eating disorders. Sancia recalls: 'Nobody noticed me at school' but 'then I lost weight/ Now I'm the size of a pea and life is wonderful.' She becomes the guru of the calorie count, consulted by her peers and revered for her strength of will. Ironically, at the very time when the body is changing and developing in ways over which we seem to have little control, the anorexic decides that here is the 'kingdom over which [they] are sole ruler'. The victims of eating disorders react to the all-too-frequent adolescent belief that one's body is (unlike everyone else's) odd, ugly, or unattractive, with a rigid effort to control, dominate and even punish that body. 'From now on you are under arrest'. Punishing the body is a concrete way of externalising the emotional and psychological anxieties which are too difficult to deal with. It can also be used as the scapegoat for all our failures. It is only when Sancia ceases to focus on food and weight and starts to look at her 'mind and soul' that the obsessive behaviour of her eating disorders begins to be addressed.

Sancia's struggle to become whole is an extreme distortion of the primary struggle of every young person to find themselves. 'I'm not here. There's nobody here,' she cries at one stage. The associated need to gain emotional independence from parents can involve intense rejection on the part of the child, whether the parents deserve it or not. 'See what she's doing to me?' asks Sancia, blaming an over-solicitous mother for her failure to lose weight.

The major concern in the play is, of course, the issue of control. The need to control one's own life and behaviour is a perfectly natural part of the process of maturing – a part with which adolescents can easily empathise. For the anorexic, however, the struggle can produce a distorted set of behaviours and emotions. If not healed, this silent, sinister 'madness' can lead not just to the darkness of an isolated tower but to oblivion itself.

LANGUAGE

Wendy Harmer has used the full spectrum of language and form to express ideas and feelings and to capture the reality of Sancia Robinson's experience. Her comic skills enable her to parody popular and recognisable forms and jingles from television and advertising – 'Two all-beef legs/No neck'. The dialogue realistically reflects the patterns of adolescent speech and slang, as in 'She won't eat anything fattening, der brain' and 'I am... a waste of space', but also draws on other idiom such as the jargon of the counselling world. Sancia can imitate facile banalities with ease as she claims to be reaching her 'inner child' and feeling 'enabled' and 'empowered'.

In contrast to this vernacular, Harmer also employs poetic forms in sections of the play. Images from childhood (fairy princesses 'locked in towers', bulimia as 'The Beast') and of food and animals abound. She sees herself as a pig 'sitting up to the trough with little trotters on the table'. Harmer's language bubbles with onomatopoeia and alliteration: 'Bag of jelly bean belly'.

The play most often draws on colloquial language, however, both to reinforce belief in the events and the character, and to reach out to the expected young audience. Harmer captures the rhythm and pattern of everyday speech with ease, using it sometimes with a cutting satirical effect as when she describes the 'beautiful people' as 'super creatures', aliens who arrive 'as small children from another planet'. In this example the pervasive influence of media images, logos, programme titles and jingles on language is also apparent. Experience itself becomes labelled like the episodes in a television programme: 'Bingeing with Sancia' and 'After the Binge'. Harmer cleverly plays with all these disparate elements of language and works them into the fabric of the monologue.

CLASS WORKSHOPS

ONE
The play begins with the actor gazing into a mirror. Use this as the basis for a mime in which you depict a range of emotions in response to what you might see when you gaze in a mirror. You might portray delight, admiration, arrogance, self-satisfaction, surprise, despair or disgust. Allow your performance to move subtly from one emotion to another.

TWO
In pairs: A and B. A begins this mirroring exercise by taking up a stance and facial expression which B then copies. B then must slowly dissolve into another stance and facial expression while A tries to move with B as

if they were mirror images. Hold the image. Then A will use a slow dissolve, mirrored by B, to another image. Try to find as many reflections as possible. A discussion about being in control or being controlled by someone else could follow after the exercise.

THREE

Alter ego. In this play Sancia's mind often speaks to the rest of her body as if they were two separate identities. In pairs enact a scene in which an individual is tempted to do something or has to make a decision. One player shadows the other and acts as the voice in the mind of the character. Another version is to use *two* players as the mind, arguing as good and evil influences.

FOUR

In groups. A number of important relationships are touched on in the play but we only see the experiences from Sancia's point of view. In role-play students could extend their understanding of the way in which the sufferer of eating disorders affects the lives of those around them. Role plays in groups could include:

- Scene at the family dinner table with both parents and perhaps other children

- Scene at lunchtime at school in which students talk about dating, dieting, and their weekend

- Scene in which students tease each other for being overweight

- Scene depicting the parents of the anorexic child consulting with a teacher, family doctor, or psychiatrist

- Scene depicting a teenager who is hiding a secret from his/her parents. The secret has been discovered by the parents who now wish to confront their child about it

• Create from five to ten frozen pictures of the most important and revealing moments in the play. Perform the depictions using a slow dissolve. Discuss the reasons for the choice of moments.

• Write your own monologue as
  * Sancia's mother
  * Sancia's friend
  * One of Sancia's teachers
  * The psychiatrist

Perform the monologue, which should be about five to seven minutes in duration. Try to use different elements of language and movement. Choose the style of acting, or a variety of styles, appropriate to the character and the point of view

• Write and perform a monologue depicting a character undergoing changes in behaviour or making a decision

• Create a collage as a chorus of voices commenting on Sancia's story. Where might you place this in the play?

• Sancia experiences many emotions in her attempts to face up to her illness. In groups depict these emotions as an abstract shape, add movement one by one, and repeat the movement using a sound or word each time the movement occurs.

NOTE:
Discussions of anorexia and bulimia can be very confronting, and should be treated sensitively. A balanced understanding of the wide range of influences which may cause eating disorders should be addressed. While statistics suggest that the majority of sufferers are female, cases of anorexic and bulimic men do occur. The issues raised by the play are not just the concern of women. The dangers to health, the psychological effects of low physical self esteem and the pressures of

social acceptance are issues of general concern. The exercises which are suggested above should be completed/attempted with close supervision by the class teacher.

THE BODY IMAGE

What is the meaning of beauty? Newsagencies are filled with magazines exposing various wonder diets. Our bookstores have shelves of texts telling us how, why, and where we should lose weight.

To break free of the constricting stereotypes in which women and men are so often still placed is difficult, and a play such as *What is the Matter with Mary Jane?* helps us to understand these stereotypes. Individuals need to peel away the layers of false and unrealistic images of themselves. Perhaps by doing so, they may find a self that they actually like – a real self, not something created by the beauty myth.

Today, to be thin is to be attractive. It is unfortunate that in today's society, the image of being thin is often seen as the prerequisite for being attractive. Ask women about weight and three out of four will state they are naturally prone to being overweight. Weight obsession is a common clinical disorder. Regardless of the fact that it is normal for women to carry more body fat than men, the sad fact is that women who are their normal body weight are often seen as overweight. For a woman, a few extra kilos can have a profound effect on her general sense of self esteem, yet approved body size and shape are simply a matter of social convention and fashion. What seemed beautiful to Leonardo in *La Gioconda* or Rembrandt in his model for *Bathsheba* would not perhaps appeal to modern male eyes in the same way. Physical beauty really does lie in the eyes of the beholder and changes of taste make it a very fragile and passing quality. Bodies make statements; therefore eating disorders can be seen as a form of communication – a way of expressing one's feelings about oneself, and about others. What are people suffering from anorexia and bulimia trying to say?

In some societies, greater weight conveys an impression of strength. A large person is hard to ignore, and in many cultures a person's weight is a measure of their wealth and their value. In other, colder, climates, body weight is an element of survival. In contemporary Australian society the opposite pertains. Fat people are failed people in the common view, the butt of humour or the object of pity. Frequently too, obesity (or the perception that one is obese) can mean that the sufferer blames their body size for all the other failures in their lives. Failing to achieve is caused by their unattractiveness and obesity – not by any other inability. It is just useless to try to change things. Failing to 'control' the body becomes the scapegoat for failing to control one's life.

Anorexia nervosa has the highest mortality of any psychiatric illness, the majority of victims being female. It is a complex disorder, with social factors being 'blamed' to a certain extent for its cause. Often anorexics are seen as seeking beauty, not rejecting their femininity, but emphasising it by becoming thinner and 'lovelier' than anyone else.

Unfortunately few adolescent females realise that 30% of their body is naturally made up of fat, in contrast to only 15% in males. Their perceptions of why they gain weight differ from male perceptions also. Males often attribute weight gain to having excess bone and muscle, and therefore as being desirable. Females on the other hand, all too frequently attribute their fat to overeating and respond by feeling disgusted with themselves and going on a diet.

The irony of the whole situation is that 'anorexics are hungry, often starving themselves to death. They want to eat, but their fear of eating is greater than their fear of death.' (Levenkron, S. 1979, in Freedman, R., London, 1986, p.160.)

Bulimics experience similar traumas, being driven it is suggested, by the need for success and the need to be attractive. They will binge on thousands of calories, then purge themselves through vomiting or laxative abuse. Ridding themselves of the associated guilt creates a vicious cycle in which bulimics find themselves trapped.

SOME RECENT STATISTICS

Source: STC program for What is the Matter with Mary Jane?

- One in every 200 Australian girls between the ages of fifteen and nineteen is affected by anorexia nervosa.

- Bulimia nervosa affects up to 10% of young women, and up to 85% of women fall into the broad category of 'disordered eating', being at some point in their lives obsessed with weight and body image.

- One in ten young people diagnosed with an eating disorder is male.

- Estimates of death vary from 3% to 25% according to the different lengths of follow-up studies

- Approximately 25-50% of anorexics regain their symptoms following treatment

- Some patients spend most of their lives in a cycle of recovering from, and becoming, anorexic

THE REVIEWS

Read the reviews reproduced on the following pages and discuss them.
- What was the *general feeling* about this play?
- Which elements were most praised?

REVIEW #1 (from the *Telegraph-Mirror*)

   a) Do you agree that this play offers 'no answers'? Are there any answers?

Reviews of the Sydney Theatre Company production, March 1995. Review #1 from the Telegraph Mirror (below) by Julietta Jameson, Review #2 from the Sun Herald (below right) by Pamela Payne and Review #3 from the Sydney Morning Herald (right) by Stephen Dunne.

The heart of the matter

ANY woman who has ever had a moment of bad self-image and any man who lives with the consequences of the late 20th Century obsession with skinny women will probably find something to relate to in What Is The Matter With Mary Jane?

It is a journey into one person's "quiet madness"; Sancia Robinson's real-life descent into the depths of anorexia and bulimia.

It was only six months ago the 30-year-old Robinson, anorexic since her mid-teens, confided her tale to Harmer.

Harmer turned it into a one-woman play and encouraged her friend Robinson to perform it.

It is the freshness of Robinson's experience, the honesty with which she has expressed her story and the playwright's intelligent sympathy for women's negative self-image that makes Mary Jane the powerful and confronting piece of theatre that it is.

Of course, there are plenty of laughs. Wendy Harmer playwright is the same person as Wendy Harmer comedian and radio personality and, naturally, she brings her style and experience to this piece.

But she combines techniques of stand-up comedy with pure dramatic interpretation.

The result is a balance between humour and pathos, accessibility and intensity used successfully to portray the important signposts along the road of Robinson's journey — her lies, obsessions, lack of sociability, self-flagellation, irrationality, sickness, hospitalisation, her turn to bulimia and final-one-day-at-a-time recovery.

---

theatre

What Is The Matter With Mary Jane? Written and directed by Wendy Harmer, performed by Sancia Robinson. At the Sydney Theatre Company, Wharf 2, until March 18.

It might be argued that What Is The Matter With Mary Jane? involves the audience in a kind of therapy session in which Robinson's very personal sickness is workshopped.

It is true, this is an intimately individual piece.

But what saves it from being self-indulgent is the universal truths it speaks.

Anorexia, bulimia, and indeed, the tragedy of negative female self-image, are usually very private anxieties.

Mary Jane offers no answers but it brings a frightening illness out of the closet, displaying its gruesome consequences for all to see.

What Is The Matter With Mary Jane? is part of the ICI-STC Education Program, aimed at school students. It is also in collaboration with the Sydney Theatre Company's New Stages program, which is involved in the research and development of new theatre works.

As part of these two agendas, the play is highly successful, giving Harmer's unusual style an opportunity to be developed, and providing a window into anorexia and bulimia that might at least get some super model-obsessed teenagers thinking.

— JULIETTA JAMESON

The
THEATRE
BY STEPHEN DUNNE
What Is The Matter With Mary
Wharf 2, March 3

THE actor is look herself in the She's squeezing a face a mask of concentration, when she the audience staring at he embarrassment is acute.

"Uh ... hi," she say Sancia Robinson, I'm 16 ye and I'm a size 10, but tha because I know I should b 8." A few moments later lambasting her physiqu hates her bum, claimi enormous, a veritable "bac bus bum". There's only on in the whole world bigger t bum — her stomach.

None of this is true. Ro body is trim and she's still a today.

The point is she thinks s All her problems will be r she believes, if only she little more weight.

What Is The Matter W Jane? is a Theatre In E piece exploring eating disc specifically anorexia nerv bulimia nervosa. The play title from an A. A. Mil about a girl who mys refuses to eat her rice p

In our world of catwalk models and toned himbos, where, de increasing obsession with perfection more and mor

Urg

6What is the m with Mary Jane She's crying w her might and main.9

WITH this childho Sancia Robinson on a journey to blighted side of her W looking glass.

This is Robinson's c given shape, theatrical m

ıma of eating disorders

. . Wendy Harmer's script has a wonderful sense of visceral humour.

oming overweight, it's no
that — according to the
ı — 85 per cent of women
e an eating disorder at
int in their lives.
er cent of young people

diagnosed with eating disorders
are male.

The central motif of Robinson's
story is control. A pimply, confused
adolescent, lacking in self-esteem
and confidence, possesses one

arena over which she has absolute
mastery — her own body.

Occasionally *Mary Jane* verges
on the harrowing, but Wendy
Harmer's script has a wonderful
sense of visceral humour, which
should appeal to a schoolkid
audience.

"Oh well, can't go out," says
Robinson, sitting on her toilet,
flicking through a copy of *Supermodel.* "Might as well throw back
a packet of Laxettes and have a
great night in!" Another segment,
Bingeing With Sancia, starts out in
high comic mode — "It's not so
important to chew this, because
we want it to come up in solid
chunks back home." Six or seven
regurgitations later, with the aid
of a fridge full of food and a
blender, the trauma of bulimia is
becoming painfully real.

Robinson is an effective and
appealing performer. Occasionally the shifts between comedy
and drama were less than seam-
less, and there's a fairy tale
princess metaphor that doesn't
work, but generally this monologue is well-paced, confronting
and engaging.

.It's also a searingly honest and
personal piece. Robinson says she
got over her own eating disorder
only six months ago, after seeking
professional help.

If this piece can help spare others
the hell Robinson and Harmer
entertainingly show us, then it's a
very worthwhile enterprise.

● What Is The Matter With
*Mary Jane? runs at Wharf 2 until
March 18. It is sponsored by ICI.*

powerful message

**THE MATTER WITH
NE?**
director: Wendy Harmer
erformance: Sancia

atre Company's Wharf 2

by writer-director Wendy
It's a story of eating
anorexia nervosa and
rgeted at that audience of
: teenagers, most particu-

on's performance is

dynamic, engaging, technically
sharp. And it's overwhelmingly gen-
erous: she flicks aside the curtain, lets
us peer into her Horrorland.

Although she uses her own name
— plays herself — this production is
no encounter group, show-and-tell
testimonial. Nor does Robinson play
the victim. She stands just to the side
of her younger self: ironic, or
exasperated, or coolly analytical, or
challenging, or ragging — always
affectionate.

Her physical energy is prodigious.
She's very funny. And she pulls no
punches. Her communication is
direct, without posture. She draws

her audience into her world, strips
any vestige of glamour or harmless
fad from the "small, quiet, submissive madness" that is eating disorder.

I have scant sympathy with the
notion that plays for youth must
propound some worthy message or
moral. Why isn't the shared experience of theatre with all its excitement
and wonder enough?

But here is a production that has a
powerful and urgent message for
teenagers. This is one story that must
be told. Robinson and Harmer are
the women to tell it — with
intelligence, veracity and, to boot, all
the excitement of theatre.

REVIEW #2 (from the *Sun Herald*)

    a) Look at the title 'Urgent, Powerful Message'. Is this an effective headline?

    b) Is this play only targeted at a 'high-risk audience' – that of teenagers? If so, what theatrical elements of the play indicate this?

    c) Could only a woman write/tell this story, as the review suggests?

    d) Does this subject work on the stage? Would it be as effective as a documentary? Why/why not?

REVIEW #3 (from the *Sydney Morning Herald*)

    a) Is the central motif, as suggested by Stephen Dunne, 'control'? What does Sancia seek to control?

    b) Does this script only speak to 'schoolkid audiences'? Does the wording of this phrase imply that the play is trivial?

    c) Does this performance work as a monologue? What are its strengths and weaknesses?

- Once you have read and studied the play, write your own review looking at the elements of review writing. Select an audience and using one review as a guide, try writing your review in the same style.

TERMINOLOGY

Find the meanings of the following words. It is important you have an understanding of these words to help you to appreciate the text .

anorexia nervosa
appetite suppressant
bingeing
bulimia nervosa
death
denial
diuretic
diarrhoea
eating disorders
emaciated
empowered
identity
illusions
isolation
laxatives
malnutrition
narcissism
obesity
purging
self-esteem
side effects
vomiting
will power

DISCUSSION TOPICS

- What are your perceptions of someone who suffers from an eating disorder like anorexia nervosa or bulimia?

- Do you know anyone suffering from either or both? Describe them. How did you know that they were suffering from them?

- Have you ever not eaten something because you were 'Watching your weight'? Do you know what your 'correct weight' should be? Did you really need to be watching your weight?

- What did you learn from reading this play? What aspects of eating disorders did you not understand before, but feel a little clearer about now?

- How important is someone's perception of him/herself?

- Are males just as susceptible to Anorexia and Bulimia? Why do you think this is so?

- Do you know what your safe body weight is and how it is measured?

- How do you feel families and friends cope when a member of their family is suffering from these disorders?

- 'It's all about control.' What in fact are people controlling when they suffer from Anorexia and Bulimia?

OTHER TOPICS AND ISSUES

The following topics are interesting starting points for discussions/ classroom debates. In addition, students might conduct some research (individually or in groups) into the following areas:

1. The 'disorder' concept. Are anorexia nervosa and bulimia diseases? What makes you think so? What medical evidence can you find to support your opinion?

2. The body image and how the media impinge on it. Choose four magazines aimed at various age groups and describe what they suggest about weight and body image for both males and females.

(Remember that there are a number of 'male' magazines on the market these days.)

3. The gentle art of advertising. Analyse a series of ads from a variety of magazines, e.g. *Dolly, Cleo, Cosmopolitan, The Women's Weekly, New Idea, Vogue, She,* etc. Choose five advertisements which aim for different audiences, and see what kind of female images they portray. Are the images positive ones? What kind of body image do they present?

4. Obesity – what is it? How much is the concept of being over-weight culturally defined rather than medically defined?

5. Dieting or DIE-ting? What does this word-play conjure up in your mind?

6. Causes of eating disorders? What do you think are the causes of eating disorders? Are there any solutions?

7. What might make some people more susceptible to eating disorders? Why?

BIBLIOGRAPHY / REFERENCES

A) BOOKS/JOURNALS

BALL, J., & BALL, R., *Eating Disorders: A Survival Guide for Families*, Doubleday, Sydney, 1995.

BALL, J., BUTLOW, & PLACE, F., *When Eating is Everything*, Doubleday, Sydney, 1995.

BRUNCH, H.: *Eating Disorders, Obesity, Anorexia, and the Person Within*, Basic Books, New York, 1973.

FREEDMAN, R., *Beauty Bound*, Columbus, London, 1986

JONES, A., & CRAWFORD, A., *Shadow of a Girl,* Penguin, Melbourne, 1995.

ORBACH, S., *Fat is a Feminist Issue*, Basic Books, New York, 1982.

SLADE, R., *The Anorexia Nervosa Reference Book*, Harper & Row, London, 1988.

TOUYZ, S.W., & BEUMONT, P.J.V. (eds.), *Eating Disorders: Prevalence and Treatment*, Williams & Wilkins, Sydney, 1985.

WOLF, N., *The Beauty Myth: How Images are Used Against Women*, Vintage, London, 1991.

Issues for the Nineties, Vol.24, ISBN 1 875682 26 0, On eating disorders (bulimia, anorexia nervosa), bodybuilding and steroid use.
Spinney Press, Balmain, NSW 2041. Tel: 02 555 9319

B) VIDEO

The Famine Within
Directed, written and produced by Katherine Gilday.
Running time 89 min.
Released by Ronin Films, PO Box 1005, Civic Square ACT 2608, Tel: 06 248 0851

C) FOR INFORMATION OR HELP RELATING TO EATING DISORDERS:

Eating Disorders Association Helpline
Tel: 01603 621414
Special Youth Helpline
Tel: 01603 765050

Provides information, help and support for people affected by eating disorders and, in particular, anorexia and bulimia nervosa. EDA is a national charity and offers a wide range of services which include a U.K. network of self-help and support groups, a telephone counselling programme for people with bulimia and a comprehensive range of information and leaflets for young people including lists of treatment available around the country.

Anorexia and Bulimia Care
15 Fernhurst Gate
Aughton
Lancashire
L39 5ED
Tel. 01695 422479

Is a Christian organisation which aims to help and support people with anorexia/bulimia and provides a list of resources, help sheets, tapes and books, including a recommended booklist. However, if you are not interested in the Christian aspect you will simply receive straight-forward. information sheets.

Childline Helpline
Tel: 0800 1111

Offers confidential help and support to young people in any kind of trouble and provides someone to talk to 24 hours a day.

WENDY HARMER is one of Australia's best known comedians. She is a veteran of the Edinburgh, Montreal and Glasgow festivals and has worked extensively in London, America and Ireland. She is the author of two books, *It's A Joke, Joyce* and *Love Gone Wrong*, and the play *Backstage Pass*. Wendy was host of the ABC TV series *The Big Gig* and in 1990 she had her own chat show *In Harmer's Way*. In 1993 she joined Sydney's 2-Day FM radio station to lead the Morning Crew. She has also written for a number of Australian magazines and currently writes a weekly column for the *Good Weekend*.

SANCIA ROBINSON graduated from NIDA in 1988. Her theatre credits include *The Tempest* (MTC), *Ring Around the Moon* (STCSA), *Abingdon Square* (Belvoir St), *The Diver* (Toe Truck), *The Glass Menagerie* (New England Theatre Co.), *Prin, I Hate Hamlet* (Marian St) and *Shakespeare's Magic* (Bell Shakespeare Co.). She has appeared on television in *Blue Heelers, Janus, A Country Practice, English at Work* and *Language Arts* and her film credits include *A Symphony of Sorts* and *Voices*.